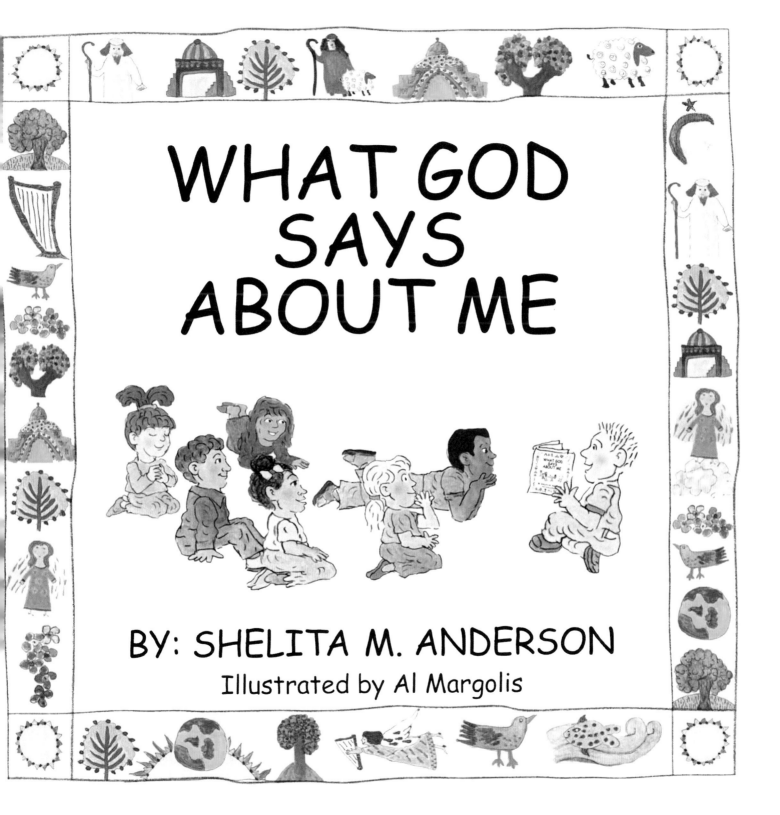

WHAT GOD SAYS ABOUT ME

BY: SHELITA M. ANDERSON

Illustrated by Al Margolis

Title: What God Says About Me
Author: Shelita M. Anderson
Illustrated by Al Margolis

ISBN: 978-1-61863-682-9

For additional copies of this book visit
www.bookstandpublishing.com

Printed in USA
Bookstandpublishing, Morgan Hill, CA 95037.
4026_1

God says, I should pray every day.

I will show God's kindness in every way.

God says, I should have love, peace, and joy.

I will share God's Word with every girl and boy.

God says, through Christ
I can do all things.

I will celebrate God's love
and all that He brings.

God says, I should obey
my parents for this is right.

I will thank God for my family
and pray for them every night.

God says, I should let
my light shine real bright.

I will love God and
His Son, Jesus Christ.

God says, I am above
and not beneath.

I am strong in God.
I will not have defeat.

God says, He does
not slumber or sleep.

I will have sweet rest.
My soul God will keep.

God says, I
should not fear.

I know God's love
is always near.

God says, His angels
are watching over me.

I thank God for His
protection.
I have been set free.

God says, Jesus came
to deliver me from sin.

I know God sent Jesus
for me and my friends.

God says, I was created
to do good works.

I am important to
God's plan in the earth.

God says, He wants
me to never fail.

I will read the Bible
and listen to God as well.

God says, I can
have good success.

I will always do God's
will and give Him my best.

good success

God says, He will
meet my every need.

I will choose life
and God's way indeed.

God says, He makes me wise;
all I have to do is ask.

I will ask for God's help
with each and every task.

God says, He has given
gifts and talents to me.

I will be all God
says I can be.

I can be a doctor, a lawyer,
a writer, or a teacher,

a pilot, a judge,
an astronaut, or a preacher

an athlete, a singer,
a dancer, or a musician

a soldier, a fireman,
a policeman, or a politician.

God says, He knows my
heart and He cares.

I will be God's giver
and one who shares.

God says, He has a plan
for my life.

I was created for the
work of Christ.

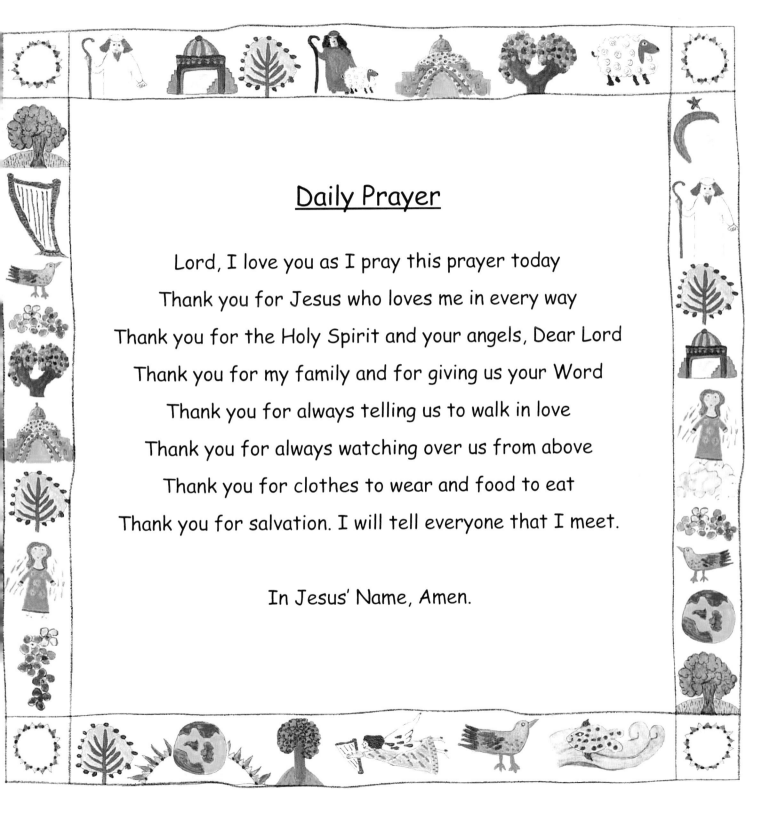

Daily Prayer

Lord, I love you as I pray this prayer today

Thank you for Jesus who loves me in every way

Thank you for the Holy Spirit and your angels, Dear Lord

Thank you for my family and for giving us your Word

Thank you for always telling us to walk in love

Thank you for always watching over us from above

Thank you for clothes to wear and food to eat

Thank you for salvation. I will tell everyone that I meet.

In Jesus' Name, Amen.

CPSIA information can be obtained
at www.ICGtesting.com
Printed in the USA
LVXC01n2034260114
370947LV00004B/5